NANTUCKET

an island sketchbook

gretchen jaeger

gretchen jaeger

winter harbor press

for MG, who made the dream a reality

Printed in the United States of America
by Cummings of Hooksett, New Hampshire
binding by ACME of Charlestown, Mass.

ISBN 0-9650885-0-2

First Edition
10 9 8 7 6 5 4 3 2 1

Winter Harbor Press

PO BOX 484, Bradford, NH 03221
    winterharborpress.com

If home is where the heart is, then Nantucket must surely boast a population of millions. The first time I stepped onto the cobblestones of Main Street, I knew I had left "America" far behind and had, in a sense, come home.

I never seem to tire of ambling about this faraway island. It seems wherever I look, I am compelled to open my paintbox. My sketchbook is actually about "remembering" and my desire to hold on to all that Nantucket means to me. I love to look back thru its pages; in the grayness of winter, I can once again be back in 'Sconset with the warm sun on my back as I painted rose covered cottages. On a long rainy day, the pink glow of a Madaket sunset can light up my whole being; and I always wish to remember how I felt the very first time I stood before the Old North Church and simply, quietly, looked up.

This is my Nantucket; dappled sunlight dancing across an old screen door, a particularly beautiful pocketful of shells from an afternoon of beachcombing, and always, always, a comforting sense of the past.

Now and then, when friends look thru my sketchbook, I'm constantly amazed how they, too, are able to recall their own island experiences, just from seeing my paintings. Sometimes, even those who have never been to Nantucket will say things like "Oh, I want to be right <u>there</u>!" I have come to realize that I enjoy sharing these little watercolors almost as much as creating them.

What you now hold in your hands is my humble offering to all who call Nantucket home, if only in our hearts. It is my love letter to an island...

bricks and cobblestones

sand and shells

roses

cranberries

hollyhocks

shingles

For an artist, Nantucket
presents a subtle yet brilliant
spectrum of hues. It's extensive
palette is constantly changing
with the seasons, the weather,
and even the time of day. Each
island color is repeated in
countless varied shades,
projecting a calming sense
of visual unity.

hydrangeas

sky

moods of the sea

moors in summer

whales

fog

moors in autumn

The Macy House, 99 Main St.

Madaket-Dionis

Macy-Howden &
Oldest House

Old Mill-Old Jail
Mona Mitchell II

Main St. Nantucket

SPRING

April and the island explodes with daffodils and the promise of warm days ahead.
Sleepy bees bumble about during the day and pinkletinks serenade in the night.

gull island lane

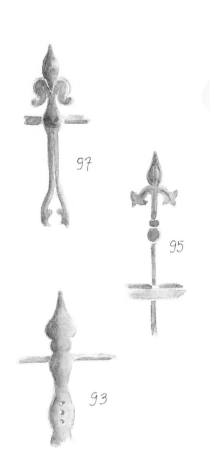

97

95

93

Three Bricks for Three Brothers, Main Street

STARBUCK	Matthew Starbuck +	Wm Starbucks
west	*middle.*	*east*

1840

Northern extremity of the Townsmeridian line

ATTENTION CHIEN BIZARRE

if you can't jump over...

TRIS

Tristram gets ready for his daily perambulation

·ANTIQUES·

ivory hair combs
embellished
with scrimshaw

1830

sailor's valentine

vintage island
postcards

petticoat
Row
CENTRE ST.
NANTUCKET

chinese
ginger jar

heirloom
cameo

One can only imagine the delights shop windows
of old Nantucket must have held, from fine Chinese
silks and porcelain to the latest bonnets from London.
I'm sure even a prim Quaker eye enjoyed an
innocent glance now and then!

MY GIFT TO THEE

jagging
wheel

too new   just right   too old

of Shingles &
Shades of
Nantucket Gray

While the Quakers may not have approved, a subtle touch of fancy can be found here and there in the usually plain lines of shingles.

GRAY LADY

a.m.   noon   p.m.   dusk

Nantucket is often called the "Little Gray Lady of the Sea"; but I'm never sure if it's due to the abundance of weathered, shingled houses or because of the fog that can so easily envelope this tiny island.

January

february

march

april

may

June

July

August

September

October

November

December

This china tea set has been in my
neighbor's family for generations.
While away on a whaling expedition
in 1830, their great great grandfather
purchased the set for his soon to be
bride back on Nantucket. To insure it's
safety, he had it wrapped in a piece of
ivory silk, which later became her
wedding dress.

How wonderful to hold a piece
of history while having a
good 'gam' over a cup of tea!

out for a row

tennis at the Casino

remembering the glory days

picking daisies on the way to 'Sconset

Summer
Nantucket 1910

a successful rantum scoot

tending the guinea hens

our cottage

acrobatics

enjoying a squantum to Wauwinet

FERRY TO NANTU

Nantucket will forever be linked with
the sea, and evidence of its Nautical
heritage can be found all over the island,
sometimes almost hidden, as Nature
strives to reclaim its own...

Altho one of the shortest, No lane beckons or
lures you into it's past more than tiny Stone Alley.
It is at once a study in textures: Holly and ivy
intertwine to form lush drapery, while underfoot,
sharp crackles of clamshells in between age worn
cobblestone snap to your attention. Weathered
shingles, crisp white fencing, the magical time
tunnel of trees as you Navigate the hill;
and the shock of reality as you
        re-enter the present...

STONE

Stone Alley.

17

CHATHAM

ESSEX

·LYDIA·

Evening glow along old North Wharf

Wisteria Lodge, Hussey St.

A little antique photo, a flea market find no less, has hung for many happy years in my home. Its identity was lost to the past, or so I thought. Imagine my surprise as I rounded this corner and walked right into my picture!

hydrangea

the elusive shades
of Nantucket
blue

a Late summer's
evening

FO'CAS'LE

Women on the island gather
and dry the blossoms, then fashion
them into beautiful wreaths.
If you're lucky, you can sometimes
purchase them at the produce carts
on Main Street.

A ship adrift on a sea of blue

madaket, afternoon

madaket, sunset

a giant, exotic shell, nestled into
an herb garden, makes for an unusual
birdbath. I wonder if whaling captains
brought back similar shells to
delight their
families?

a dainty
wreath of
mussel
shells

catch of the day

channeled
whelk

scallop

My pockets are always full of shells when I return from the beach. I'm quite certain that the ones I found today are prettier than the ones I found yesterday, and tomorrow's will be prettier still. Who can resist such treasures?

slipper shell

jingle shell

moon snail

mussel

the moors

cranberry bogs

NANTUCKET

produce carts, Main St.

HARVEST

scalloping

LEFT BANK

1772

CASTLE BANDBOX

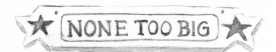

NONE TOO BIG

FISH HOUSE

MIZZENTOP

SWEET PEA

COMPASS

HEART'S EASE

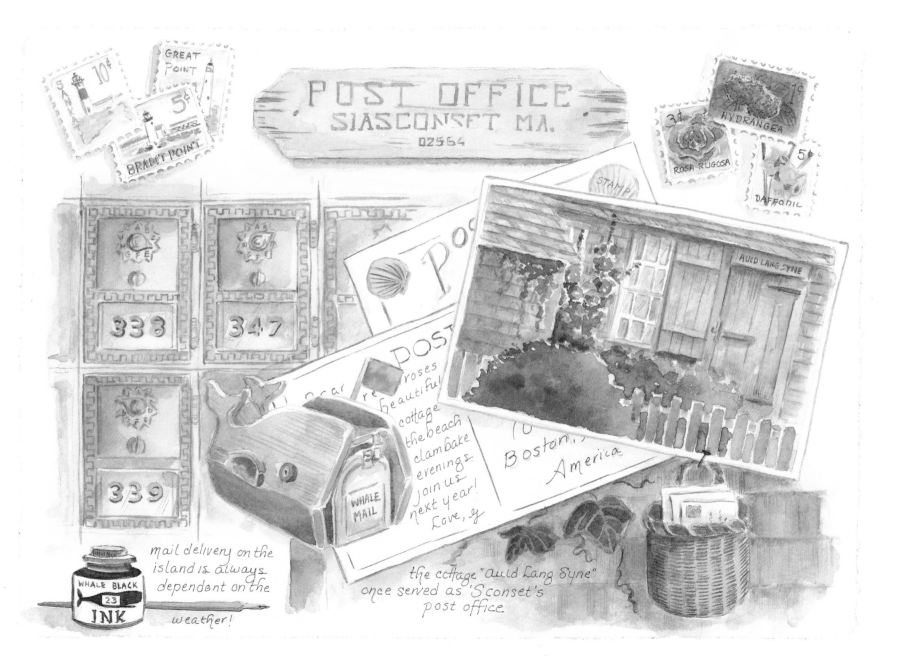

POST OFFICE
SIASCONSET MA.
02564

GREAT
POINT
10¢
5¢
BRANT POINT

3¢
HYDRANGEA
1¢
ROSA RUGOSA
5¢
DAFFODIL

STAMP

333

347

339

AULD LANG SYNE

WHALE
MAIL

Dear
roses
beautiful
cottage
the beach
clambake
evenings.
Join us
next year!
Love, y

To
Boston,
America

WHALE BLACK
23
INK

mail delivery on the
island is always
dependent on the
weather!

the cottage "Auld Lang Syne"
once served as 'Sconset's
post office

"Behold how Good and how Pleasant it is
for Brethren to Dwell Together
in Unity."
~verse inside
'Sconset Chapel

The Old Mill

a stepping stone into the past

CORN MEAL

FINEST NANTUCKET QUALITY

Nantucket's Life Saving Museum is quietly Nestled into Polpis Harbor, also a safe haven for Numerous species of birds especially during migratory Seasons. Seems we humans were Not the first to find renewal of spirit on this tiny island.

Iris identifies a blue heron

scrollworker's whimsy
a sea serpent perhaps?

methodist church

summer house

milestone marker

weather vane

up for the season

window of old gaol

off Union St.

bull's eye glass

boot scraper, Main St.

chimney of "Oldest House"

mortgage button, Pacific Bank

the bug light "CYC"

I was made on Nantucket
I'm strong and I'm stout
Don't lose me or burn me
And I'll never wear out

—verse inscribed on
bottom of antique
lightship basket